ROCKSTAR SPA

spa leadership guide

Ainslie Colless

A practical approach to Spa Management.

A guide to support Spa Therapists in progression of their Spa Career, highlighting an advanced understanding in the multifaceted role of Spa Manager.

My goal

To give Spa Managers tools they can incorporate into their daily practices while empowering the talented Spa Therapists they work with, for increased effective work practices in the Spa environment.

#spaon

A brief history of spas

"Spa is no longer a niche industry, but instead is a major revenue producer for the hotel industry. Food and beverage, as well as accommodations revenue, can be substantially complemented by spa and wellness revenue streams."

— Bryan McGoldrick, Managing Director and CEO, Global Brands Australia

The word 'spa' has many meanings. It is seen as an acronym for salus per aqua, in Latin meaning 'healing through water'. The original use of a spa was as a thermal bath or spring, where mineral-rich spring water was used for its medicinal properties. Another theory is that the term 'spa' comes from the town of Spa in Belgium, where water treatments are popular.

From bath towns in Roman times to the destination spas we are familiar with today, the concept of a spa is to heal or improve one's lifestyle in a relaxing and recreational setting. Wherever they are located, spas have always been recognised as a sacred place of healing.

From what was a slow evolution as it wasn't seen as vital, the spa concept now is a multi-billon-dollar industry incorporating various techniques. Spa Therapists are able to utilise up-to-date training and treatments to enhance their offerings for results-conscious consumers.

Health and wellness – the business of being well – is not a luxury but a basic need for a happy life. Western culture would benefit from reflecting on Indian culture and their five needs of living:

- Health
- Family
- Friends
- Faith
- Wealth

Luxury lodge spas introduced the value of health rituals in daily life, where spa professionals have the ability to make the world a better place, one spa session at a time. Daily rituals allow health to naturally occur. By seeing it as a way of life, everyone is able to have a 'spa life'.

3100 BC **300 BC**	Egyptians used water and herbal remedies.
1000 BC **546 BC**	Earliest writings of Chinese Medicine. Balneotherapy Thalassotherapy: Therapeutic treatment involving bathing in sea water. Hydrotherapy, treatment of maladies from use of water.
700 BC **200 BC**	Greeks practised cold bathing rituals for wounded warriors
460 BC **370 BC**	Hippocrates suggested the cause of disease is due to imbalance of bodily fluids.
200 BC	Hebrews practice purification ceremonies through floating in the Dead Sea.
27 BC **14 AD**	Bathing in Greek and Roman Times. Bathing protocols of modern times based on these settings. Romans baths were bigger than Greeks, however they did copy many of their practices with baths becoming popular for social use.
43 AD	Romans developed "Aquae Aulis", a spa in Bath in Britain
11th C.	Spas becoming more popular, people begin to visit in need of cures of various maladies.
1326	Collin Le Loup discovers springs of Spa, Belgium. Resort is built around natural springs, which lead to spa meaning any health based resort surrounded by natural springs, which would benefit particular ailments.
1556	Different cultures produce variations on spa from Japanese Ryoken, Turkish Hammam, Saunas in Finland.
16th C.	First scientific book published "Compendium of Materia Medica", highlighting benefits of thermal baths and tonics use, written by Pharmacologist Li Shizhen. Royal visits increased popularity of spas.
1700s	Mineral water is seen as beneficial taken internally as well as eternally. Mrs. Elizabeth Farrow discovered a stream of acid water running from a cliff through the coastal town of Scarborough

Physicians in Germany, Italy and England saw medical use of spring water, recommending spring waters for treatment of ailments.	**18th C.**
Vincenz Priessnitz establishes first modern hydrotherapy spa with health package treatments combining fresh air, cold water and diet and exercise in Germany.	**1829**
Modern massage as we know Swedish Massage is developed by Physiologist Per Hendrick Ling.	**1806**
Holistic Herbal water therapy developed by Sebastian Kneipp (Kneipp Therapy) Public baths across Europe experience spread of plague and syphilis due to incorrect usage; many were closed.	**1890s**
Elizabeth Arden opens The Red Door, Manhattan's first Day Spa, offering manicures, pedicures and facials	**1910**
Deborah Szekely opened first destinations spa, Rancho La Puerta, in Baja California. Golden Door Spa launched in California, incorporating weight loss and fitness regimes.	**1958**
California launches newest trend, the fitness spa, The Ashram.	**1974**
U.S. Spa services introduce medi spas, where therapists work alongside doctors in luxury spa settings.	**1997**
Increased popularity for spas. No longer just for wealthy women, but for all looking for a healthy lifestyle, with increased male consumers.	**2000**
Oldest Roman Spa located in Merano, Italy is still available for use. Return of trend of Flotation tanks Cutting-edge techniques used to deliver evidence-based, results-driven treatments for skincare. Luxury biopsychosocial treatment, for anxiety, depression and pain	**Today**
Mental Wellness Return to Indigenous techniques.	**Future**

"The challenge of leadership is to be strong, but not rude; be kind, but not weak; be bold, but not bully; be thoughtful, but not lazy; be humble, but not timid; be proud, but not arrogant; have humour, but without folly."

– Jim Rohn, American Entrepreneur, Author, Motivational Speaker

"Great leaders don't set out to be a leader They set out to make a difference. It's never about the role – always about the goal."

– Lisa Haisha, Life Coach, Speaker, Author

RockStar Spa Manager:
(Noun)

An emotionally intelligent spa professional who is driven by excellence in their efforts to encourage others to increase their efforts to sustain workplace goals and performance. They motivate others with their ability and passion for their craft and make things happen through their engagement of the human connection.

Spa Managers should be excited about the possibilities of the evolution of the spa industry and how we can influence change and growth within our spa, ultimately allowing consumers to infuse spa life into their lifestyle.

Data released from the Global Wellness Summit (20 October 2016) provides figures detailing how the spa and wellness industry is of the world's largest and fastest growing industries, despite an economic downturn. Data states the spa industry has grown from $94 billion to $98.6 billon from 2013 to 2015. 2020 data shows that the Spa and Wellness industry has grown to $4.5 trillion. Ophelia Yeung, Senior Research Fellow (GWI), predicts consumers will continue to spend big on wellness due to a growing subset of consumers who are seeking experiences rooted in meaning, purpose, authenticity and nature.

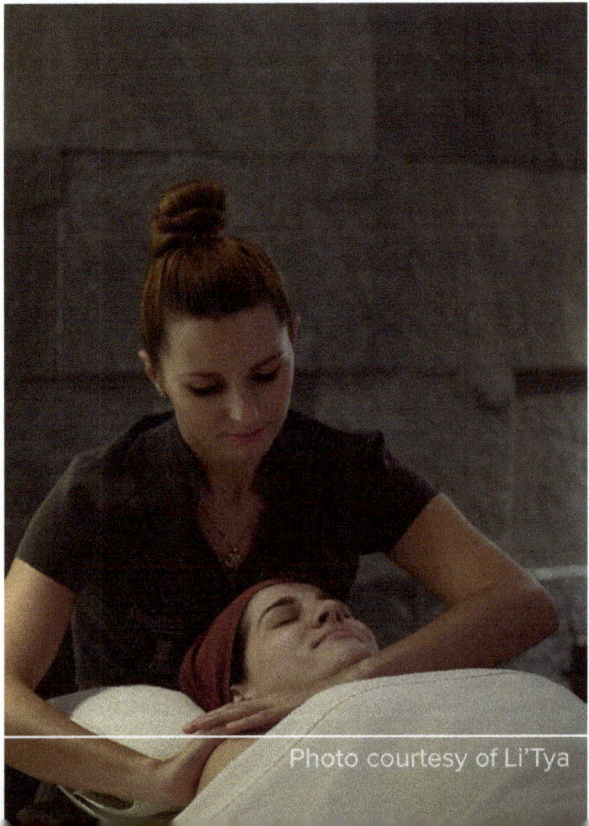

Photo courtesy of Li'Tya

A RockStar Spa Manager should:

- Have spark

- Be excited to perform spa treatments

- Be self-motivated and engaging

- Be up to date with industry news, and keep their team informed

- Realise that you don't need to know everything or have all the ideas, just recognise a good idea and acknowledge others for their knowledge

- Be clear on expectations

- Give feedback constantly; don't wait until the 6- or 12-month performance review

- Give credit when credit is due; people need to feel appreciated

- Learn to let things go. Pick your battles; some things will annoy you, but will it really matter tomorrow?

- Act and not react – if you need to remove yourself from a situation before you act on an issue then do so

- Be realistic; goals and tasks. Be aware of how therapists like to work

- Assist with therapists' goals

- Be thankful to your team

- Always end the day on a positive note.

- Be unpredictable. Every now and then tell a spa member to jump on the massage bed and give them a 1/2-hour massage. It's great for them to know you are awesome at treatments too.

RockStar Spa

The reliance on three fundamental basic elements is required for a successful spa dynamic, which are shown below and which we will be looking at in this book.

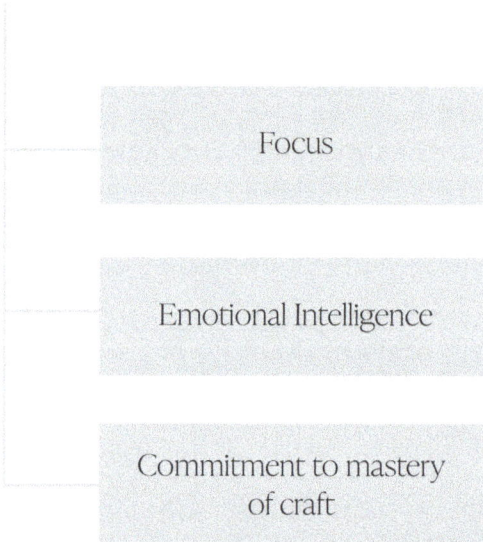

Focus

Emotional Intelligence

Commitment to mastery of craft

"A goal without a plan is just a wish."

– Antoine De Saint-Exupéry, French Writer

Photo courtesy of Spa Kinara, Longitude 131°, Baillie Lodges

Creating your plan of attack

The chapters of this book act as a guide to an overall plan of action to build and maintain your own RockStar Spa. It is designed to be dog-eared, jotted on and marked with your own maps and plans through its pages. Or if you are reading the ebook, make sure you take notes as you read.

You'll see on the following page that a plan has already been started for you, as an example. Feel free to use this as the starting point for your own plan.

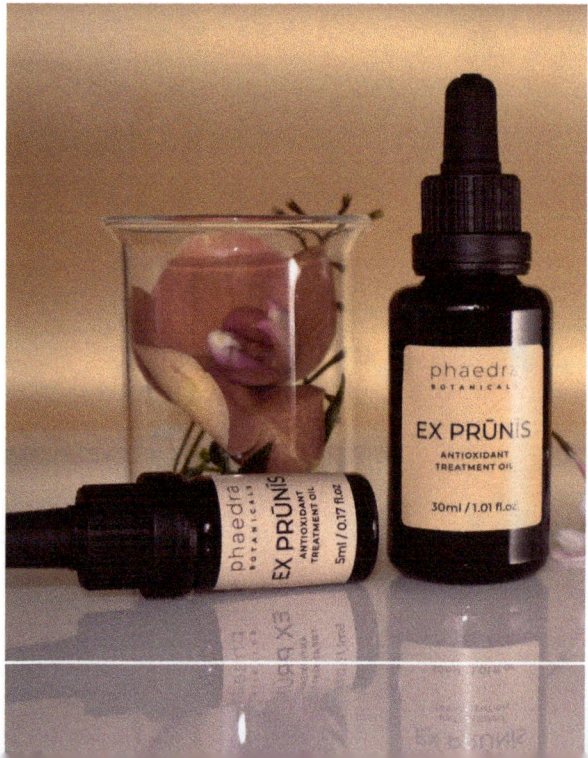

How to build a RockStar Spa

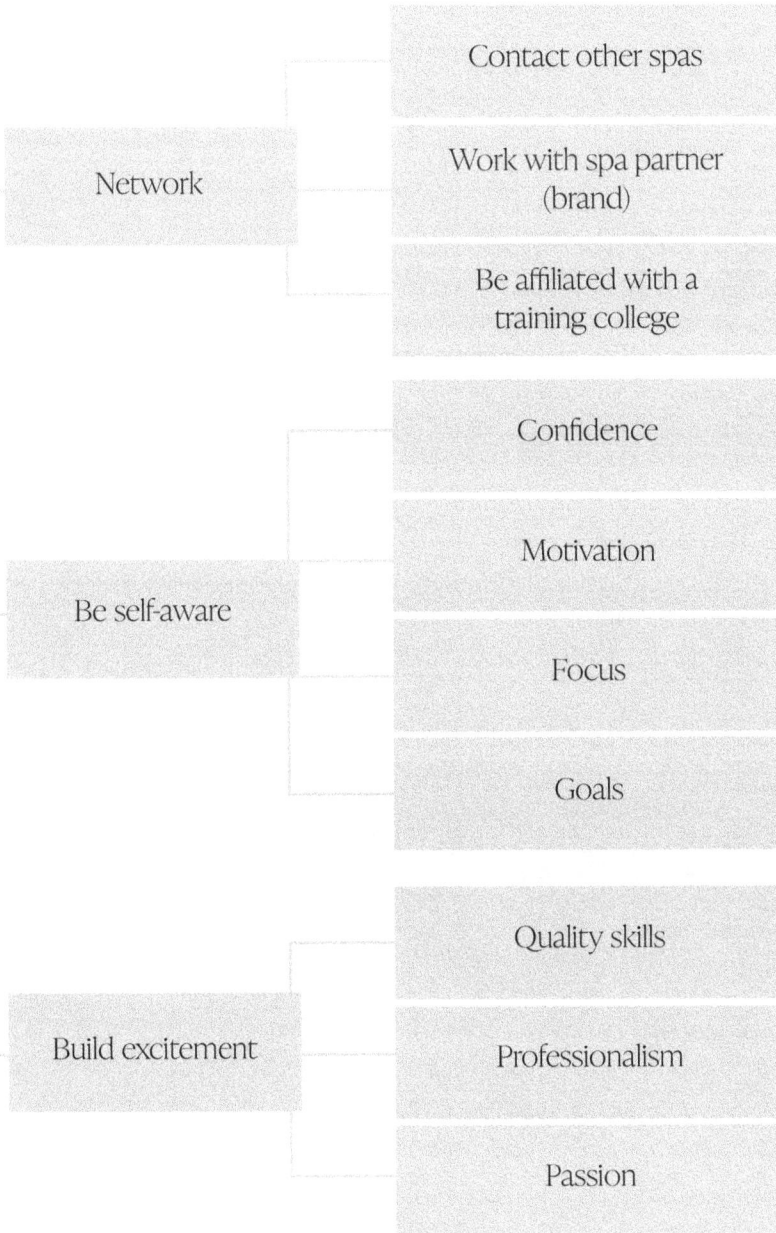

Network	Contact other spas
	Work with spa partner (brand)
	Be affiliated with a training college
Be self-aware	Confidence
	Motivation
	Focus
	Goals
Build excitement	Quality skills
	Professionalism
	Passion

Your plan for success

The Plan For Success Flow Chart is a map that is designed to support managers with long-term operational effectiveness. While each team has its forming, storming, norming and performing cycle, it is also important to be aware of how you are going to motivate your team to work at an optimum level, understanding that there may be bumps along the road. The Plan For Success Flow Chart should be used as a tool to reflect on what you need to implement at each stage of progression, and when interruptions occur.

PLAN FOR SUCCESS

- UNDERTAKE SELF-DEVELOPMENT
- HIRING OF THE RIGHT PERSON
- GREAT WORK ENVIRONMENT
- CREATE GOALS, COMMIT TO KPIs
- CONDUCT SELF-DEVELOPMENT
- IMPORTANCE OF RETENTION
- UNDERSTANDING TRIGGERS
- TEAM BUILDING EXERCISES

Photo courtesy of Li'Tya

Action plan

Undertake self-development
- Session with mentor
- Pinpoint any addition qualifications required
- Maintain daily rituals for balanced lifestyle and perspective

Ensuring hiring of the right person for each role, driving engagement through excitement and experience
- Commit to SOPs and values
- Let therapist see you a person

Create a great work environment

See chapters:
- Seeing the bigger picture
- Spa mise en place
- Continuing education
- ExSPAtations
- Communication
- Spa operation

Utilise:
- Group activity: build a team that cares
- Activity: build a spa community
- Daily spa operations checklist
- Spa amenities and tools checklist

Create goals, commit to KPIs, challenge to strengthen each therapist	See chapter: • Goal setting Utilise: • Goal setting template
Conduct staff development	See chapter: • Building high-performance teams Utilise: • Rockstar development program • Luxury spa performance indicators
Understand importance of retention	• Understand importance of retention • Consider impact on budget of continued hiring and orientation training practises
Understanding triggers of employees planning to leave:	• Learn to recognise signs of therapist being uninterested in work practices: complaining, burnout and mentioning other places of work
Conduct team-building exercises	See chapter: • Building high-performance teams

Why do you want to be a Spa Manager?

Before going any further, it will be really helpful for you to think about why you do what you do. Understanding where you are now will help you get where you want to be.

Things to ask yourself:

- Why do you want to be a Spa Manager?

- Why are you a Spa Manager?

- What do you want to achieve?

- What are your goals?

Use the chart below to start considering your goals. Draw your own chart, and adjust the pie accordingly, increasing sections of higher priority to you. You can also add in your own goals.

Goals

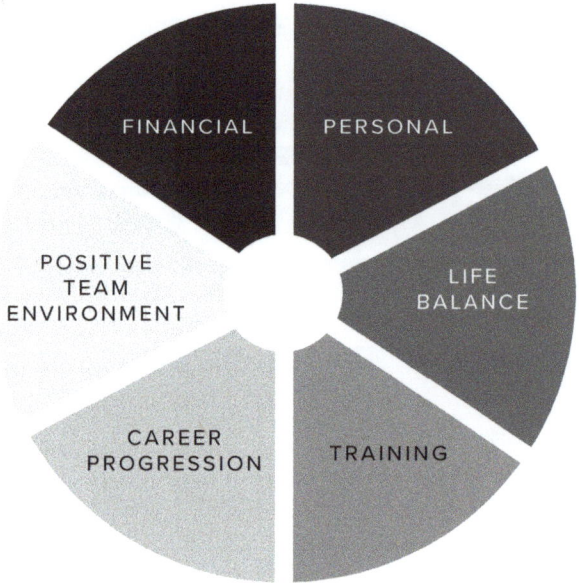

- FINANCIAL
- PERSONAL
- POSITIVE TEAM ENVIRONMENT
- LIFE BALANCE
- CAREER PROGRESSION
- TRAINING

Photo Courtesy of Southern Spa, Southern Ocean Lodge, Baillie Lodges

Who am I?

Take time to consider your current style, and create a
mind map starting with the below and then adding in
points that are relevant to you. (If you're not sure what a
mind map is, there are several online that will give you
inspiration: (www.micro.com/templates.)

- People skills
- Strengths
- Weakness
- Working in a team

- Networking
- Influencing
- Communication
- Organised

What is my personality type?
How will that affect my role?

DISC Management profiling can be found online. This is a
tool that will give you insight to your personality type.
www.discprofile.com
www.discpersonalitytesting.com

Qualifications

- What additional qualifications do you need to help you
  reach your goals?
- What do you want to achieve as a manager?
- Note any networking, further information,
  or mentoring needed:
- What is your plan to focus on your weaknesses?

Personal leadership styles

Leadership is not only about influencing others and driving them to succeed, it is about handling ideas, your ability to make decisions and how your prioritise your action lists. Here is a simple outline of leadership styles to guide new managers who are required to organise people and task management.

Authoritarian leadership (autocratic)

This leadership style is the highest level of control. Often it is seen used by someone who seems bossy, using short and sharp commands; it is designed for use for an area which requires absolute government. This is useful for operational standards and policies to ensure organisation and discipline. This style is also useful in situations of high pressure, as no contribution or ideas are sourced from others in order for the work to proceed.

Participative leadership (democratic)

As the name suggests, this style allows for participation from team members to facilitate problem solving and ideas conversations. It's ideal for increasing the standard of service, where flexibility is needed to facilitate particular guest needs. For it to be successful, a high level of communication is required as well as respect of other team members' ideas.

Delegative leadership (laissez-faire)

A more laid back approach, a laissez-faire style means a highly skilled and experienced team can be left to make their own decisions. This style not only requires a high level of trust of the team members but the manager is required to ensure they have given them the competences to perform the tasks, the resources required and the authority to complete tasks.

Leaders can also be:

People orientated
Trainer – increase effectiveness moving forward/ invokes a community feel

Coach – support, performance can decrease in managers' absence

Task orientated
Hands on – when training, orientation, for team members low in experience

Hands off – highly skilled team, experienced

Micro-manager
Oversee all fine details, constant supervision

Macro-manager
Goal orientated, sees the bigger picture, allowing team to make smaller decisions
Spa leadership

Spa leadership

For successful outcomes you will find that the different leadership styles are required at different times. During the various stages of on-boarding, training and day-to-day procedures, different leadership styles are required. For example – using the Authoritarian Style when planning an event will not give the team the feeling of being included and may limited their willingness to be involved.

Orientation and training
Authoritarian leadership (autocratic)
- Quick decisions
- Provides clear expectations
- No need for creative input from trainees
- Autocratic style also used when team members confused, uncertain or inexperienced

After training stage and SOPs and standards are met
Participative leadership (democratic)
- Stresses and increases teamwork while increasing performance
- Allows Team Members to be proactive and problem solve
- Team members become more motivated

Delegative leadership (laissez-faire)
- Highly skilled/experienced therapists can be left alone to get on with their tasks after clear communication of role, SOPS and goals
- Works well with motivated staff
- Knowing when to be hands off; less input from manager if the team is working well and achieving goals

Events and creating new spa experiences
Participative leadership (democratic)
- Guidance
- Allow input from Spa Team
- Higher quality of contributions from the Spa Team
- Spa Team feel they are involved, the spa belongs to all Spa Team
- Motivated manager has final say

Busy times
Authoritarian leadership (autocratic)
- Clear communication
- Quick decisions
- No creativity required
- No room for suggestions or opinions from the Spa Team

Photo courtesy of Aore Island Resort

Case study:
Spa manager speal

At regular intervals ask therapists, "What is your favourite product?" It gives time to discuss your product line, reflect on treatments and guest outcomes they have seen while using products, and the ingredients they enjoy using. This can act as a segue to discussing the ingredients and their benefits within the treatments they are performing and how they can recommend home care use.

It is motivating for therapists to know about other spas and therapists and new treatments that are available. A sharing task can involve a therapist researching information on new technologies and presenting to the team.

While it is easy to plan and train a team when you are motivated yourself, reflect on the difficulties that can arise when you are flat and positivity is low.

Consider a time that you haven't been positive or motivated towards a goal or task. This can happen at any time to anyone. The key is to have a strategy to gain balance and get back on track.

List activities where you feel positive and regain your motivation:

Positivity	Motivation
✓	✓
✓	✓
✓	✓
✓	✓
✓	✓
✓	✓
✓	✓

Creating your mission statement

The creation of your own mission statement is the driving force of the focus of the Spa Team. The idea is to have a standard that the team is proud to be a part of and create a brand culture for the work environment. It should be something that your team can relate to and aim to accomplish every day.

- Create: consider what you want your actions and delivery to say about your spa

- Share: allow your Spa Team to understand how they are involved in the delivery and what it means to achieve your mission statement

- Achievable: how will you know your mission statement is achieved?

- Measure: allow for feedback from guests and therapists to evaluate if your mission statement is achievable, valid and valuable

- Synergy: individual team members will be excited and motivated to be apart of something bigger than themselves

RockStar Spa mission statement

Guests take time from busy schedules to visit RockStar Spa, therefore their treatment time is of high value. All guests should receive a memorable experience, not just 'spa treatment'. The quality of our Spa Experiences is what makes RockStar Spa stand out from other properties and sets a benchmark for other luxury spas.

Example of Mission Statement

"To provide a memorable Spa experience for all guests that sets us apart from all other Spas."

Criteria to note:

- Spa touches
- Warm hands
- Quality of touch
- Not breathing over guest
- 'In the moment' – here and now with our guest
- Spa speak: intonation and pronunciation
- Does the treatment feel bespoke or repetitious?
- Walk the floor like you own it and welcome guests into your space with confidence
- Ask yourself: how am I going to enhance my guests' life with my treatment?

"Leaders must be close enough to relate to others, but far enough ahead to motivate them."

— John C. Maxwell, American Author, Speaker and Pastor

Photo courtesy of Li'Tya

Seeing the bigger picture

Managers need to set healthy boundaries– to be understood by but not personally involved with your team. In her book The Four Mindsets, Anna-Lucia Mackay outlines critical points on emotional intelligence and how it benefits a team and a manager aiming to motivate them.

A key trait of effective managers is self-awareness. Your self-awareness, or ability to self-manage, is how you manage your interactions with others, depending on situations and settings.

An emotionally intelligent manager is constantly looking for cues that people give through their actions, responses, body language and tone of voice. Having this information helps a manager to supervise their people more effectively, both as a team and as individuals. A strong manager has the ability to respond constructively in emotionally uncomfortable situations.

Use the questions below as a guide to start mind mapping your emotions and being in the present.

Emotional self-awareness questions:

- When was the last time you felt uncomfortable at work? Did a teammate notice?

- When was the last time you felt angry at work? Was another team member involved? How did you resolve that anger?

- When were you optimistic at work? Did anyone notice?

- When were you recently confident at work?

- When were you last inspired at work? Who was involved?

- When were you last overwhelmed at work? Did anyone notice and did they assist you in any way?

- When were you frustrated at work? What did you do?

Emotional intelligence of a RockStar Spa

Spa Therapists are known to be emotional beings, as they are caring for and giving attention to their guests. For the spa to run efficiently, individual team members are required to understand their own feelings while having empathy for their colleagues, showing a broader perspective of perceived reality for the team to maintain a steady flow.

Criteria to note:

- Trust
- Group identity
- Group efficiency, through cooperation and collaboration
- Awareness of regulation of emotional intelligence within a team
- Using experience; reflect and feedback

Team members should understand that they are a person first, a therapist second and an employee last.

All members of the team including the manager have to relate to each other as people first, then as therapists. When Spa Team Members see their colleagues as a person and see each other as equal, they will self-manage their emotional intelligence in times of conflict. All Therapists should value and share their skillsets.
As employees everyone has different motivations and goals.

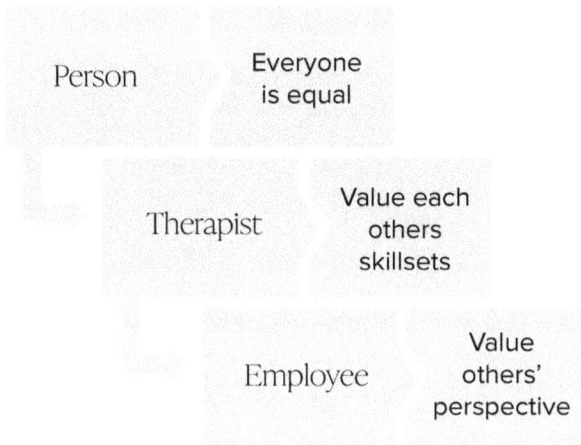

Person   Everyone
                is equal

          Therapist   Value each
                             others
                             skillsets

                    Employee   Value
                                      others'
                                      perspective

The Spa Manager's Role

Create and promote an empathetic, high-emotional-intelligence team:

- Remove ego

- Create time to talk about what is on each other's minds

- Form norms that support understanding and regulation of emotions within a team

- Use team-building exercises

- See teammates as equals that balance the spa dynamic, through exploring each others' skillsets

The Spa Team needs to relate to you has a person to feel trust, in order to be motivated to attain individual and team goals. How much of your own character you are willing to share will enable your team to engage with you and give you trust. For your therapists to fully understand and respect you as a manager, all parties have to see each other as people, before therapists, and before goals are issued and achieved.

This theory is defined in the 'Johari window', which is outlined in the following diagram. How much of yourself you are able to share with your team will enable you to be a transparent manager, gaining trust and clarity, enabling assurance that the team is on the same path and working towards similar values. It is based on the premise that trust is acquired by sharing information and learning about your self from feedback of their perception of you. The Johari window is designed you increase communication and increase understanding and training.

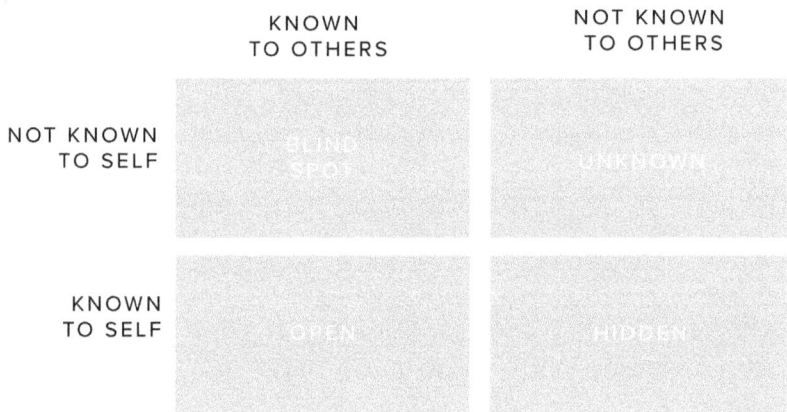

	KNOWN TO OTHERS	NOT KNOWN TO OTHERS
NOT KNOWN TO SELF	BLIND SPOT	UNKNOWN
KNOWN TO SELF	OPEN	HIDDEN

Johari window

Maslow's Hierachy of Needs is a psychological theory which clearly outlines the basic needs of humans and how they are motivated to achieve tasks.

Maslow's basic premise is that people are motivated to achieve certain needs. It is the quest of the Spa Manager to align those needs to the team's own performance goals

For anyone to have progress in their life, they need to work their way up the ladder, step by step, after having attained each individual need.

It is valuable to reflect during training if therapists have been offered all of their needs to support their goals. When situations arise of a negative nature or there is a struggle to find a connection, referring to the Spa Hierarchy of Needs on the next page is advised. Ascertain if the desirable spa space and tools have been offered for the spa dynamic to be effective.

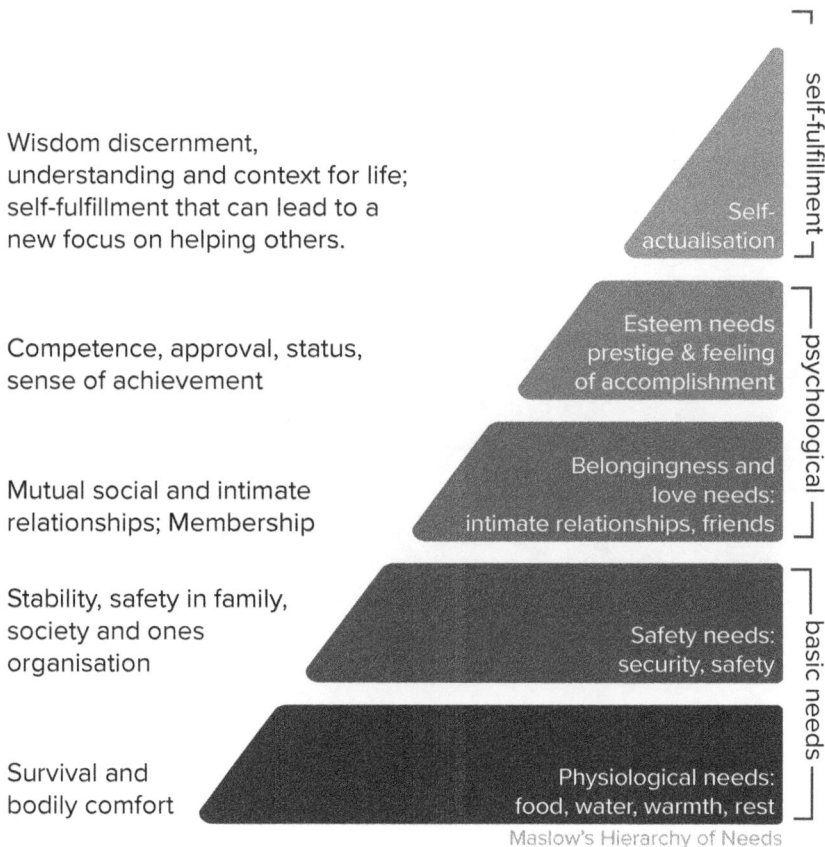

Wisdom discernment, understanding and context for life; self-fulfillment that can lead to a new focus on helping others.

Competence, approval, status, sense of achievement

Mutual social and intimate relationships; Membership

Stability, safety in family, society and ones organisation

Survival and bodily comfort

self-fulfillment

Self-actualisation

psychological

Esteem needs prestige & feeling of accomplishment

Belongingness and love needs: intimate relationships, friends

basic needs

Safety needs: security, safety

Physiological needs: food, water, warmth, rest

Maslow's Hierarchy of Needs

RockStar Spa Hierarchy of Needs

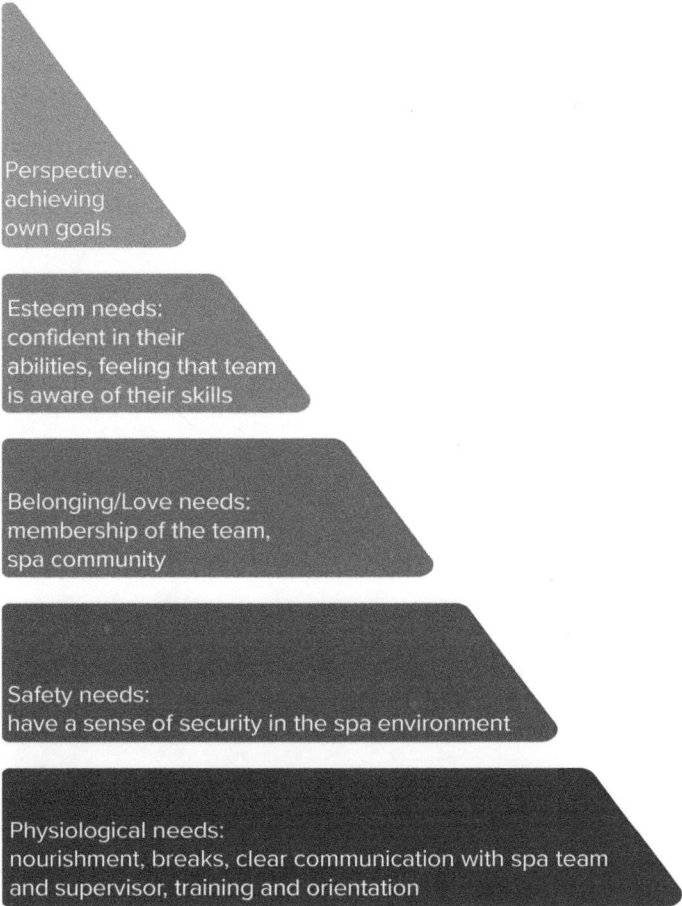

Perspective: achieving own goals

Esteem needs: confident in their abilities, feeling that team is aware of their skills

Belonging/Love needs: membership of the team, spa community

Safety needs: have a sense of security in the spa environment

Physiological needs: nourishment, breaks, clear communication with spa team and supervisor, training and orientation

Photo courtesy of Southern Spa, Southern Ocean Lodge, Baillie Lodges

Case study: An unpopular therapist

A therapist is performing to an acceptable level, however the rest of the team does not enjoy working with them. While the therapist is maintaining positive feedback from guests they are performing treatments on, the rest of the team feel negative about working with this person. This therapist also complains about working conditions, and you can see that they are constantly trying to get your approval as a manager. You are feeling drained from this therapist as they constantly require praise for their work. Consider the following:

- Does the therapist relate well to their manager?

- Does this therapist complain about the working conditions?

- Can the therapist speak openly with their manager about issues?

- Is the therapist happy with the time off they have – is it suitable for their own work/life balance?

- Does the therapist feel safe in the environment? Is it ok to make mistakes? Are they consulted in a reasonable fashion in regards to the correct standard of operation?

- Does the therapist have friends at work or feel that they are openly involved in the spa?

- Does the therapist feel like a valued member of the Spa Team and can seek and share therapy advice?

- Does the therapist feel that the team recognises the quality of their work?

- What key performance indictors or goals has the spa manager set to enhance performance or growth?

- Does the therapist feel that they are being listened to?

- Are they aware of the Spas Mission Statement and actively promote it?

- Does the therapist feel that they are given equal opportunities as teammates do within the spa?

- Is the therapist given adequate tools to achieve their own goals?

- What progression available? Is it possible for the therapist given a Specialist role within the Spa for own growth?

"I don't judge people. It blurs out the center of my attention, my focus, myself."

— Toba Beta, Betelgeuse Incident: Insiden Bait Al-Jauza

Focus: the difference between average and extraordinary

A manager should aim to instil a sense of pride among the team about their treatments, while constantly aiming to provide guests with a memorable spa journey. This is done by focusing on the individual needs of each guest while recommending lifestyle improvements through products or daily practices.

The Spa Manager needs to differentiate between manager focus and that of a therapist. This will highlight the roles and how the team will perform effectively.

Key considerations when defining role scope:

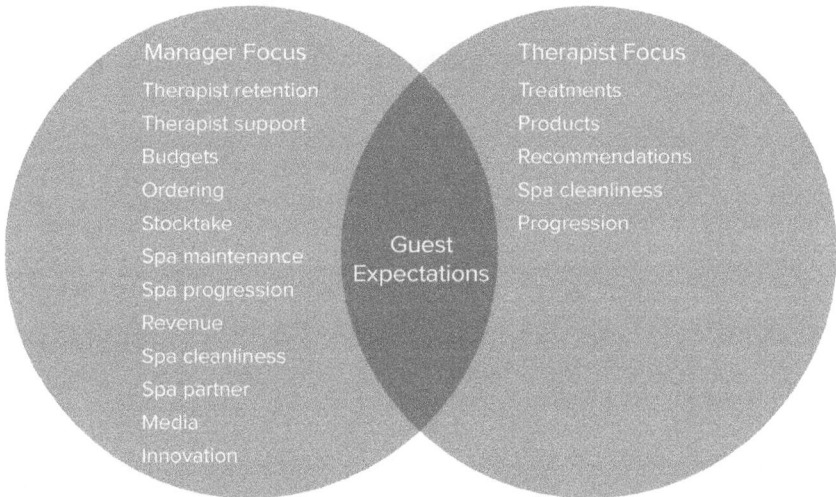

Manager Focus
Therapist retention
Therapist support
Budgets
Ordering
Stocktake
Spa maintenance
Spa progression
Revenue
Spa cleanliness
Spa partner
Media
Innovation

Guest Expectations

Therapist Focus
Treatments
Products
Recommendations
Spa cleanliness
Progression

- Tasks and responsibilities

- Performance expectations

- Required skills

- Require knowledge
- Required external training and continuing education
- Core requirements or attributes

"Organisation isn't about perfection. It's about efficiency, reducing stress and clutter, saving time and money, and improving your overall quality of life."

— Christina Scalise , Professional Organiser, Author

Spa mise en place

Organising and setting up a spa to the 5S theory makes reaching goals and targets easier, with the use of process maps and checklists while giving visual control over an appealing work environment. Remove unnecessary objects and sort the spa tools that will be used daily and store them in areas that remove excessive walking and reaching. Everyone will know where things are kept, eliminating redundant communication, as all equipment is stored in the best place to utilise space and time.

Lean Six Sigma: 5S

Taking the time to map out your plan will not only save you time, but lead to an efficient spa.
Various tasks can be considered:
- Stocktake
- Reports
- Rosters
- Orders
- Emails

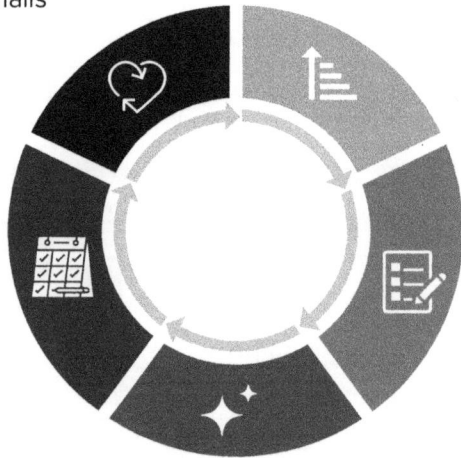

Sort: keep only necessary items

Shine: Keep area neat and tidy

Standardise: Set standards and create checklists for consistency

Set in order: Arrange items to facilitate efficient workflow

Sustain: Maintain and review checklists

Note the tasks on the calendar and mark yourself out for that time. Let your team know that this is what you will be doing. It's important that you have some alone time.

If they haven't any treatments, that's cleaning time. Cleaning is marked off on the calendar, serving as a reminder of the frequency of certain tasks. It makes the team see this as important work as part of the spa operation.

Always tell your team that administration is integral to the smooth operation of the spa and that you appreciate them doing some cleaning at that time so that you can get together and do something fun later. It is helpful to verbally outline what you are doing, and to give your team a timeline, to assure them that you are interested in working with them to improve or share skills. It is crucial for therapists to understand that their manager is achieving something when at their desk.

If you are feeling overwhelmed with too many tasks to accomplish in a short time frame, start with your least favourite. This allows you to focus more, as you move on to your most favourite tasks.

At the completion of your tasks give your Spa Therapists time to teach you something – "tell me what you know about … " You will find therapists love to teach you as well.

Allocate a resources drawer which all therapists have access to. It should include all training materials as reference, and HR forms such as incident reports and leave requests. This drawer should contain all information to run the spa, not only in the absence of the Spa Manager but it also works as an easy handover for a replacement.

Therapists who are promoted to the role of Spa Manager may suddenly find themselves having to deal with many emails. The book *Work Smarter: Live Better* by Cyril Peupion is a thorough guide for organisational tips as well effective email usage. It is a fantastic place to start.

January

SUNDAY	MONDAY	TUESDAY	WEDNESDAY	THURSDAY	FRIDAY	SATURDAY
27	28	29	30	end of month report 31	1	2
rosters 3	start performance review 4	stocktake 5	6	7	orders 8	9
10	11	12	13	14	15	16
rosters 17	18	19	20	21	orders 22	23
24	25	26	27	28	end of month report 29	30
rosters 31	1	2	3	4	orders 5	6

Timing trick

The clock can be the arch nemesis of the spa therapist and manager. The best weapon against this constant battle is having an understanding of how you spend time and working in real time. Most tasks require less time than therapists realise. Allocate time as 'treatment time'. When therapists perform a treatment for a certain allotted time, prescribe your own task for the time the treatment is to be finished by.

Also consider room turnaround time. Fifteen minutes can be a staple amount of time to complete small tasks in your to-do lists that require no other assistance to action.
Use the side bar (see below for an example checklist) to quickly mark if the tasks are urgent or important. Note that tasks can be important without having to be actioned with haste.

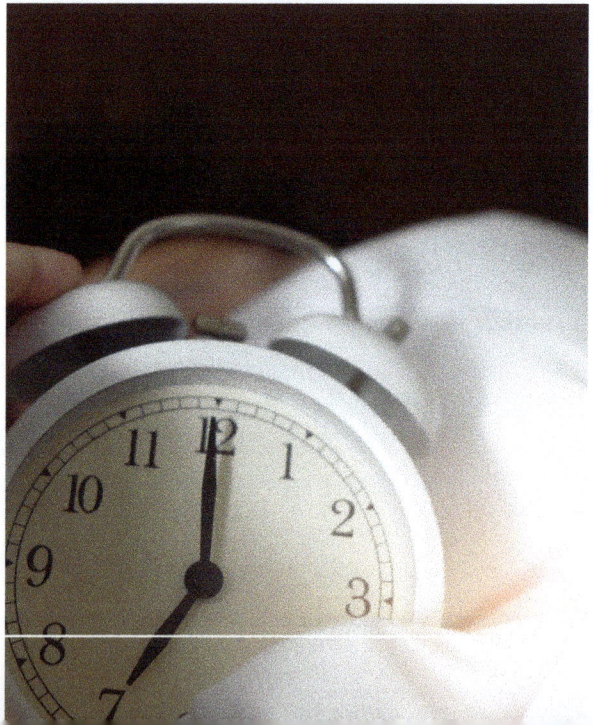

Date	Tasks to Action

15 Mins

□ Important
□ Urgent   Product check / all here in order

□ Important
□ Urgent   Quick cleaning job

□ Important
□ Urgent   Email check / action

60 Mins

□ Important
□ Urgent   Spa partner teleconference

□ Important
□ Urgent   Complete daily to-do list

□ Important
□ Urgent   Ordering

□ Important
□ Urgent   Interview new staff member

90 Mins

□ Important
□ Urgent   Linen stocktake

□ Important
□ Urgent   Product stocktake

□ Important
□ Urgent   Reports

Timing Table

Fill out your own Timing Table below to get into mindful time management habits. It can be copied and used as a daily action plan.
Note how many of your tasks are important compared to urgent.

Date	Tasks to Action

15 Mins

☐ Important
☐ Urgent

☐ Important
☐ Urgent

☐ Important
☐ Urgent

60 Mins

☐ Important
☐ Urgent

☐ Important
☐ Urgent

☐ Important
☐ Urgent

☐ Important
☐ Urgent

90 Mins

☐ Important
☐ Urgent

☐ Important
☐ Urgent

☐ Important
☐ Urgent

ExSPAtations

Therapists need to understand your expectations. These may include but are not limited to:

- Dress standards
- Etiquette
- Standards of spa procedures
- Training standards
- Education

All expectation and standards need to be outlined in an employee handbook, with all procedures included.

You need to be the example of the exSPAtations, making them doable and less of a 'task' and more of 'this is how we roll'.

Dress standards should be outlined in hiring documentation, and this becomes one of the core values for all team members.

A constant issue with exSPAtations is training standards and education. Spa leaders should be engaged in industry activity and training standards and available courses.

Continual education should be a key priority – take the time to talk with each therapist as to any further study they are interested in, and for assisting in the facilitating of time off.

"Leaders don't force people to follow, they invite them on a journey."

— Charles S. Lauer, Publisher, Columnist, Public Speaker, Mentor

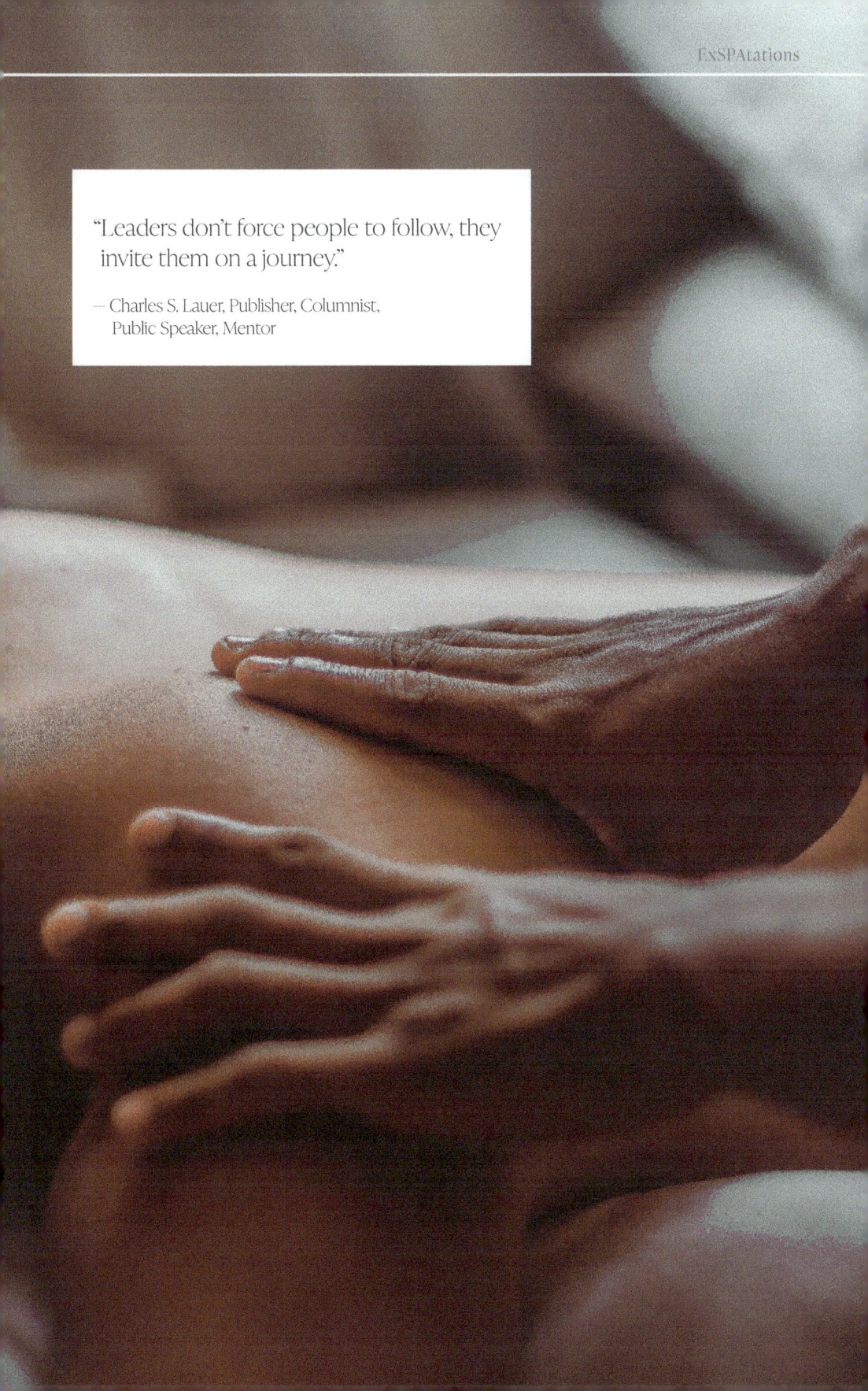

Continuing professional education

The 'trainer' style of people-orientated leadership is often cited in spas. As educated professionals, therapists are provided the resources they require to move forward and they often form a community and learn together, becoming a stronger team.

Consider issuing all therapists with their own scrapbook for their own visual aid and learning. It becomes a place to keep all tasks and spa information, and personal learning notes. Therapists are advised to use it as they please. Scrapbooks allow therapists a space to store all their spa information, with no double-handling of information, saving time and confusion.

Although scrapbooks are ideal for storage of spa knowledge, learning should be as verbal as possible. Therapists need to speak about spa menus and recommendations, not just write them.

"Education is the mother of all leadership."

— Wendell Willkie, American Politician

Learning activities

1. Consultations
   - Find main concern
   - Offer a solution
   - Explain why to use product / how to use product
   - Results are shown by a correctly delivered treatment or product used for the guest concern

2. Each therapist to be aware of common skin condition, explain how it affects the facial, the products and techniques used. Suggest home care.

3. Skin conditions
   Understanding skin conditions vs concerns
   - what to focus on
   - how condition affects facial
   - guest's main concern
   - put it into their life circumstances
   - what ingredient is doing the work
   - how to use the product especially for them
   - hero product that can be used with what they have
   - understanding guest's priorities, e.g. face or body or hands or feet
   - any information you know that will therapeutically assist them

Thought patterns for product recommendations

- why has guest booked this treatment?
- what is their main concern?
- ask and understand what they are using at home
- find the gaps
- find the priorities
- put it in their life circumstances, so they are able to actually use the product
- explain how product is used
- explain why they need it, the ingredient that is beneficial
- listen to them, and think, and have a conversation about it; don't lecture them about the benefits of the ingredients
- ask yourself – why am I suggesting this product? What action will it take? Will guest use it?

Understanding personalities

In a group setting, using advertisements of beauty products, ask, 'which of the advertisements appeals to you'. It is designed for a group discussion and they realise how different ads appeal to others in the group. Further discussion can then be focused around how different information is delivered to different personality types. Drawing from the personalities in the group, you can then move on to the realisation that each guest needs the same product, treatment information and service delivered differently to achieve positive results. Therapists are encouraged to jot notes in their scrapbooks detailing their own behavioural changes needed to benefit each personality type.

Build your own profile

Encourage your therapists to write their own 'spa biography'. Therapists need to see themselves as individual professionals. Have them take the time to define themselves as therapists, and evaluate their goals to see if they are relevant to achieving this. Researching other therapists to support their industry awareness is a key element to this task. It is not about comparing to others, but to be excited for other therapists in their roles.

Verbal quiz time:

Quiz each other on products and ingredients or spa treatment explanations during opening the spa and during cleaning sessions.

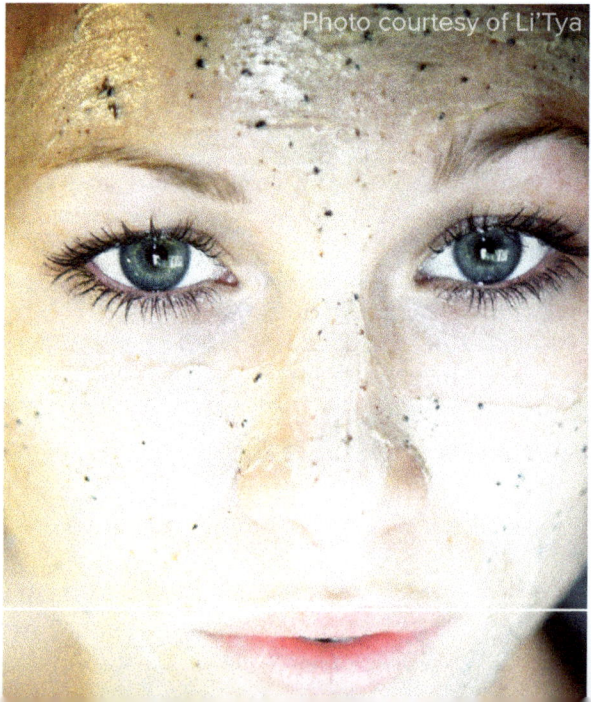

Photo courtesy of Li'Tya

Communication

Good communication includes defining what is expected from your Spa Team and how you are going to get there for optimal functioning of a high-performing spa.

With all therapists requiring qualifications as pre-requisites for their positions in spas, most Spa Managers and team members leave a lot to presumed prior knowledge. But presumption is the root of many problems in any work environment.

While job descriptions are considered a clear outline of goals and expectations, they often leave a gap for operational tasks. Simple checklists can bridge this gap.

These lists need to distinguish who is doing what and when, and how long each task is expected to take. Detail should be given in the beginning for further understanding.

New managers can often find themselves being task-minded or driving the team forward, often forgetting to take the team for the ride. Daily morning briefings can be used to outline the focus of the day, also delegating each team member jobs to do, goals and a learning task of the day.

Working within a standard of daily operation, therapists are guided to a structure which can outline ideal times for things such as questions and leave requests, and can give you better flow and less interruptions.

COMMUNICATION

+

EX<u>SPA</u>TATIONS

+

OUTLINE
THERAPISTS' ROLES

=

HAPPY TEAM

Communicating to influence

When working with others it's often noted that a person's ability to translate information can change during peak times. Your personality can affect your communication skills as well. Managers of high-performing teams differ in their ability to assess the success of their own communication within peak and low times and change accordingly. This is a learned skill, improved with much practice. Feedback from co-workers and people in all aspects of your life can assist you with advancing. The first step is to ask for feedback, while being reflective on the effectiveness of your own behaviour.

Photo: courtesy of Li'Tya

Management styles

Management Style	Context
Autocratic	Busy peak periods of spa operation use clear, short demands
Trainer	Quiet times, to allow for further explanation of protocols and spa standards. Your team will want to understand "why" and understand the reasoning
Coach	For therapists new to the industry. While this can be more time consuming, often requiring one-on-one time, the rewards can be substantial with higher performance, particularly with therapists feeling accepted into your spa environment
Hands on	When training inexperienced staff, show the technicalities of each task, to show what you are expecting
Hands off	When training experienced staff or a highly experienced team, a verbal explanation, with clear short demands, is required.

Communication task

- Practise giving directions as if you were speaking with someone with limited English. Note how direct and clear you need to be.

- When speaking with your therapists, note their body language and consider your own.

- Is it positive?

- Is it defensive?

- Is it accusatory?

- Do you have a warm and open demeanour?

- When needing to clarify, use fewer and different words. Simply repeating what you said initially isn't helpful if there was confusion the first time.

- Become aware of how you communicate with others. Do they have to ask you multiple times 'what do you mean?' or 'what did you say?'

- Internally note if you mumble, and how you intonate or pronounce words. This can lead to communication errors in busy periods.

- Formulate questions to quiz your Spa Team to test their assumptions of spa protocol. Spend time to clarify to bridge the gap in their perceptions to ensure that you are all on the same track.

- Remember: the way you communicate sets the tone of the entire spa and what is acceptable.

"Skill is the unified force of experience, intellect and passion in their operation."

— John Ruskin, English Art Critic

Spa operation

As an operating unit, the spa involves the same tasks being performed every day. The variables are the people we meet and the treatments we perform. This makes it exciting; the people we meet, and how we are able to impact their lives through our care, therapy, and lifestyle recommendations. For most therapists this is why they are involved in the spa and wellness industry and what makes it exciting on a daily basis. Having an effective operating system allows us to work with ease and enjoy our work to the fullest.

Due to layout design, area available, guest volume and therapist numbers, spas need different operations. It is advisable to take time alone in the spa and trace the guests' steps. See it through their eyes and how you want to use the space. Refer to the 5S Principle to assess the flow of the spa for the guest experience.

Open and close

These processes need to be so simple that everyone in the team can do them, and checklists are a good way for everyone to be on task.

Meet and greet procedure

All staff need to be thoroughly and individually trained on the intake of guests. The spa journey for guests also needs careful consideration.

The Luxury Spa Performance Indicators – provided at the back of this book – have been developed to clearly outline all interactions with guests, including the sequence of events.

Lists are ideal to keep on top of daily actions. Lists should be re-evaluated and tasked prioritised at the end of the day to set up the flow of the following day.

GO CRAZY, and let your therapists make decisions when you are present. It gives you an idea how they would handle operation should you be away.

Time	Action Plan
0900	**Open Spa**
	Manager:
	• Confirm daily manifest for guest information
	• Double check appointments for day
	• Ensure therapists/reception have everything they need
	• Set task for the day e.g. Retail goal, learning, share skills
	Reception:
	• Open front of house
	• Open till/check monies
	• Check cleanliness of spa
	• Print therapists' treatment schedules and present in team room
	Therapists:
	• Prep treatment rooms
	• Confirm that all product/equipment needed is in order
	• Confirm appointments
	• Check guest information
0930	First spa appointment
1200	Actions to manager inbox e.g. invoices, leave requests
1200 - 1400	Lunch staggered for therapists
1500 - 1600	Reception:
	• Confirm tomorrow's appointments
1800	Close Spa
	Reception:
	• Balance and close till
	• Close front of house
	• Report any issues to manager
	• Guest feedback to therapists
	Therapists
	• Clean up spa treatment rooms
	• Close up spa treatment rooms
	• Tidy prep room
	• Debrief with other therapists/manager on any cases of interest
	Manager:
	• Check action lists
	• Prep list action list for next day
	• Assist reception and therapist in the above
	• Quick reflection of day, ask for feedback
	• Confirm with therapists of any leave applied for
	• High five team or dance party to complete day

Daily operations checklist

Action Required	S	M	T	W	T	F	S
Open spa							

Check linen delivery

Turn on lights, music, hot cabbies

Phone checked for messages, and reply if action required

Turn on steam room and sauna

Ensure steam room and sauna has refreshments and towels stocked

Brew tea of day

Fill water stations

Amenities fully stocked in bathrooms

Plump cushions in lounge

Sweep front entrance

Treatment rooms stocked with fibrella/cotton rounds

All surfaces in treatment rooms clear of visible oil marks

BOH tidy

Appointment book checked, day printed for therapise BOH prep area

POS system turned on ready payments

Close Spa

Next day appointments confirmed

End of day report/reciepts cash up

Turn off hot cabbies, leave door open, empty trays of excess water

Turn off steam room and sauna

Spray steam with disinfectant

Clean/refresh bathroom lockers, top up all amenities, towels, combs etc.

Empty all bins

Clean and put away all equipment used

Wipe BOH benches, Ecolab green spray

Clean all teacups and put away

Turn off music/lights

Linen in bags, to BOH entrance for pickup

Lock all doors

Spa amenities and tools checklist

Action Required

	S	M	T	W	T	F	S

Amenities - from laundry

Candles

Tissues

Toilet Paper

Refill all shampoo, conditioner, bodywash.

Hand wash and body lotion whole new container, no refill

From ALM store, key required

Cotton rounds

Cotton tips

Tissue box covers - in case of breakage

Bins - in case of breakage

Tea cups - in case of breakage

Cleaning Equipment - from laundry

Mop heads

Sponges

Glass cleaner - blue spray, refill

Bathroom cleaner - pink spray refill

Disinfectant deodorizer - green spray, refill

Dishwashing liquid, refill

From kitchen

Floor cleaner

Sanitiser (for steam and equipment)

Office Supplies - from FO BOH

Brown retail bags - small

Guest collateral, media pamphlets

Guest notepads and pens

Printer paper

Printer cartridge

Case study: Tasks being missed

A therapist consistently left out operation tasks and left the team picking up after them, particularly during open and closing procedures. This resulted in management staff having to double check and often stock equipment and set rooms according to spa standards.

Before discussing with therapist, consider if they have all the tools and information required to perform task adequately.

- Create checklists of open/close procedures, to be signed or ticked daily

- Create go-to lists to ensure all staff know where all their tools and amenities are to be stocked from

- Ensure standards are available, with current pictures if applicable of room set ups

- Enforce the importance of using, completing and initialling any checklist that you have created

- Refer to company policy on acceptable workplace standards

- Ensure you are using questions to deliver understanding of workplace requirements, not just telling spa members what to do

- Put the therapist's own knowledge into practice, ensuring the reliance on their own craft

Reflection

At the end of every day take some time to reflect on the how effective your spa protocols are. Ask your team how they enjoyed the day.

Questions to prompt:

- What did you like about the day?

- What didn't you like about the day?

- What made it easier to focus on your treatments and guests?

- How does the flow of the spa affect your day? Do you find anything in particular easy or hard?

- Were there any room prep difficulties?

- Any tips to make the day easier?

"Leaders become great, not because of their power, but because of their ability to empower others."

— John C. Maxwell, American Author, Speaker and Pastor

Goal setting

Goal setting can be seen as a challenging task, but it should be taken seriously.

It can apply to current work standards, whether it is faster room prep or the way you talk to a guest to enhance your communication skills.

Give therapists time to think about their strengths/weakness and work on moving forward together. Take the time to discuss the needs of the therapists' working day, for example preferred lunchtime, room prep difficulties.

Ideally you want to aim to be the spa to change therapists' lives as much as your guests'. Aim to be the kind of Spa Manager that enhances every therapist you work with, so that while they were great before working with this team, they end their employment having the inspiration and tools to be the best therapist they can. This way a manager's work always exists, as therapists pass on their knowledge and passion to the next therapist.

Suggestions include:

- Technical skills
- Courses to undertake
- Management skills, further progression
- Where to they see themselves in six months
- What kind of therapist do they see themselves as
- Skillsets they wish to enhance or use more

It is also a way to easily discuss how long a therapist plans to work in your spa (this is ok — future planning for you).

Each therapist's goals need to be documented. Should a stage arrive when a team member becomes problematic after showing promise, their documented goals become an objective reference. Things to also consider for the recent change include:

- Working hard without praise
- Boredom
- Not enough challenges
- Lack of progression

Spa Manager Role

Manage by goal setting and evaluation of progression at regular intervals, e.g. monthly/six monthly, giving therapists timelines for targets.

See the Goal Setting Template on the next page.

Goal setting

GOAL	What I want to achieve
MEASURE FOR THIS ACHIEVEMENT	Subjective measures; facts Objective measures; how you feel about goal now
DATE TO ACCOMPLISH BY	Timeline to complete goal
WHAT WILL I NEED TO ACCOMPLISH MY GOAL	Resources, Training, Funds, Mentoring
IS MY GOAL ACHIEVABLE	Is what I want attainable, can I make this happen myself?
WHAT ACTIONS DO I NEED TO DO	1. 2. 3. 4. 5.
STEPS REQUIRED TO COMPLETE ACTION	1. 2. 3. 4. 5.

Action plans

Use an action plan to outline your management style, your goals, and your professional development.

Checklist

- Do I know my management style?
- Daily operations outlined?
- Personal goals: Monthly/ Quartly/ Annually
- Professional organisations to be a part of
- Do I have a focus?
- Do I have enough time for each daily task, or do I need to delegate?
- Do I have a spa partner that can work with me?
- Do I need a mentor?

Use the space below to map your processes

Building high-performance teams

Spa Teams can be defined by product theory. Consider your team as a cosmeceutical product. Cosmeceuticals enhance the appearance of the skin's surface by having a therapeutic effect on the skin. It's about looking at the cell structure and function below the stratum corneum. We are concerned about the activities below the surface.

Trained therapists and some consumers are aware of active ingredients through various forms of media, all advertising new technologies for the best penetration of products to enhance skin health and appearance. A high-performance product does not rely on active ingredients alone. To have the desired results active ingredients need to be utilised long enough for them to be delivered to target sites to gain the desired effect.

While it may seem ideal to maintain a team of 'active ingredients', various elements are required to maintain a balanced and well-functioning team.

The ideal is to remove and dispel free radicals, which can have a serious effect on individual team members. They contain a high electrical charge, being very unstable and very reactive, ultimately creating situations that may destabilise and damage an entire team.

"You can do what I cannot do. I can do
what you cannot do. Together we can do
great things."

— Mother Teresa, Saint

A strong manager must act as an antioxidant and defuse the situation, as a positive enzyme. The trick is to be like an antioxidant and not be stressed, let go of personal emotions and remove negative energy. Antioxidants self-destruct as they attract oxygen and in turn stabilise free radicals, which can be the example a manager can use. Remove ego and let go of the damaging free radical.

Often characteristics that work well together are preservatives and emulsifiers. Preservatives ensure the safety and stability of the team while emulsifiers avoid separation during formulation (forming, storming, norming, performing). They work to keep the team balanced and together harmoniously.

Team members with flavonoid properties are anti-inflammatory, often diffusing times of tension or keeping a calm state with their medicinal nature. Flavonoids are supported by protein, with their eliminating of inflammation potential and focus on regeneration. They can be a strong backbone for any team, as they present in a mature or experienced therapist.

Gelling agents can be the least active, so teamed with other components they provide body and contribute to the overall feel of the team. The value placed on the gelling agent can strongly control the outcome of a quality team.

In the same way as cosmetic ingredients, spa members should undergo vigorous selection to ensure they last and are capable of achieving the required results while maintaining minimal disruptive periods.

While team members will have their dominant trait, all need to be regarded as an active ingredient and given the opportunity to perform at peak levels. Like the ingredients of cosmeceutical products, all team members are required to perform their own function in order for the product to be balanced and complete.

By now you should be thinking about how the skillsets are interrelated to your goals and how you wish to achieve them.

- Do your therapists have enough knowledge to build rapport?
- Are treatments performed to your standard level?
- Are products being recommended by therapists?
- Are product recommendations made with confidence leading to sales?
- How does each therapist's "Ingredient Component" affect their ability to perform?

The graphic below highlights the relationship between the three fundamentals criteria continually spoken off. The stronger the customer service and rapport with guests, the better the flow on effect it has on the therapist's ability to confidently recommend products and rebook treatments. Use it in conjunction with Spa Team ingredients to reflect on the results currently given by your team, and consider if the "ingredients" have an effect on the team dynamic and the individual ability to perform.

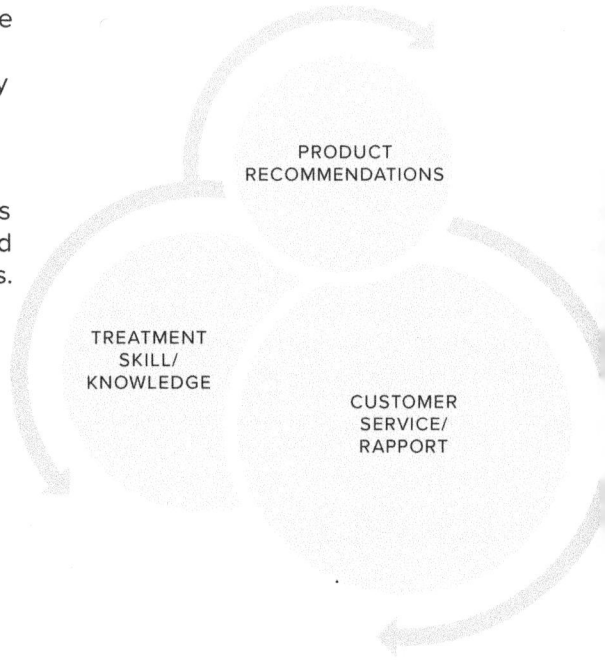

Jason Fox discovered performance motivation can be reflected in game theory. He found that gamers were motivated to complete their game by having external optimism to complete a task, which had measurable results. To move through the various levels of games, gamers required commitment to the mastery of their craft (the desire to be better and beat the baddies in the games) to complete a challenge. Games provide intense feedback, allowing for a rich experience for gamers, therefore increasing the gamer's performance.

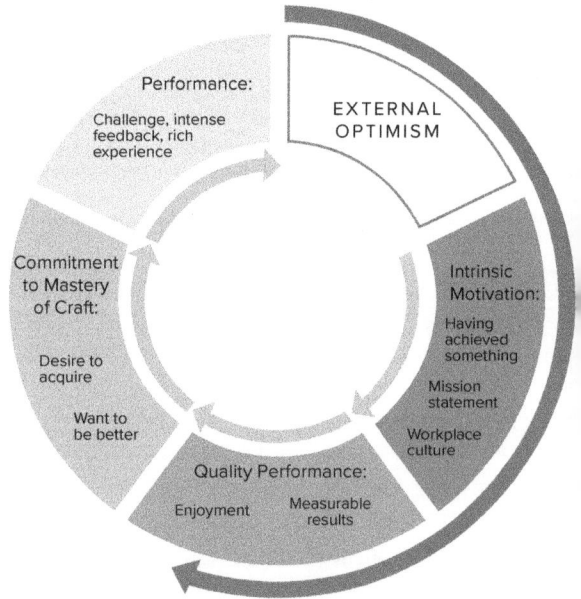

Spa Managers should keep this in mind when building high a performance team and managing each team member.

PRODUCT RECOMMENDATIONS

TREATMENT SKILL/ KNOWLEDGE

CUSTOMER SERVICE/ RAPPORT

Performance:
Challenge, intense feedback, rich experience

EXTERNAL OPTIMISM

Commitment to Mastery of Craft:
Desire to acquire
Want to be better

Intrinsic Motivation:
Having achieved something
Mission statement
Workplace culture

Quality Performance:
Enjoyment   Measurable results

Group activity:

Build a team that cares

The below matrix is an example of a tool that can be used as a platform for new team members to bond and get to know each other. It is also great for new managers to see how the team goes about the task to see how they fit together.

All team members can be given a copy of the matrix below, or use your own that applies to you. Each therapist needs to fill out all of the questions, for other members of the team. Include therapy-related questions to give therapists an idea of the skill sets that surround them. This allows for building trust in colleagues' skills and interest in each other, and is a recommending basis for referral for treatments, to ensure that the guest receives the best possible experience from the most appropriate team member for their individual needs.

AREA OF BODY I SPECIALISE IN MASSAGING	SPA TREATMENTS THAT I ENJOY PERFORMING	HOW LONG I HAVE BEEN MASSAGING FOR/ORIGINAL QUALIFICATION
SPECIALISED MASSAGE CONDITION OR TECHNIQUE I AM INTERESTED IN	FAVOURITE AREA OF BODY TO HAVE MASSAGED	LEISURE ACTIVITIES I LIKE
ESSENTIAL OILS/S I LIKE	MY NEXT HOLIDAY WILL BE...	IF I WEREN'T A MASSAGE THERAPIST I WOULD BE...

"A 'just a job' employee does just enough to keep their job while complaining about what's not fair or right at work.

"A 'team player' works positively together with everyone to get the job done the best way possible.

"See the difference?"

—Ty Howard, Motivational Speaker

Manage Performance

One of the major differences between a Spa Therapist and a Manager is the Manager is constantly considering areas for innovation and improvement. Not only is the emotionally intelligent manager analysing their own performance but that of the team and its individual parts.

Bring attention to the need for a desired skill — Are therapists aware of those they don't possess?

- Do they know what is required of them?
- Do they know the value of it?
- Do they know why their performance matters?
- Are they aware of any incompetence?

Coaching is a highly targeted, goal-driven approach to analyse and identify areas to address and to develop required skills and behaviours to increase performance. The MEDIC model can provide guidance to spa managers aiming for corrective solutions.

Motivate
Educate
Demonstrate
Imitate
Consolidate

Performance management plans are appropriate for poor conduct, bullying, harassment, discrimination, drugs, policy breaches, damage or theft, and inappropriate behaviour.

Spa Manager's role

- Give each therapist praise for their role in the spa
  Define how their role and strengths benefit the team
- Gradually give learning activities to strengthen other areas of their role
- Use strategies to address unconscious incompetence, through buddying, re-training, or shadowing
- Ensure all therapists are confident in all operational tasks
- Give therapists mind mapping processors for solving problems
- Implement MEDIC Model

A RockStar Spa Manager sets tasks through challenges to gain experience to improve competency with all tasks.

CHALLENGE	• Goals set
STIMULATION	• Explore: how to make it happen
REWARD	• Outcome/ complete ideas • Take action

Case study: RockStar therapist

Every now and then, someone in your team has to be a rock star.

There will be a busy day or group of guests that one therapist will be more suitable to look after and you should embrace this. Team members come with their own knowledge and experience, and in some cases languages, which become a benefit to the guests' experience.

An example: A group of German guests arrived, speaking little or no English. The team were all of different nationalities and fortunately one therapist was fluent in German. She did more treatments than anyone else and also interpreted for others between treatments, allowing a higher level of service to be given to each guest. A long and hard day for one therapist, although support from the rest of the team meant she felt like a rock star, instead of being overworked.

Reflecting on the RockStar Hierarchy of Needs, consider what fundamentals made the scenario successful:

- Therapist felt skillset valuable to the team's success

- Therapist was given support from team

- Therapist was given appropriate breaks due to support of team

- All team members worked in synergy to achieve the mission statement of the spa, overall feeling positive and motivated

Creating your Spa Community

Creating your spa community is not limited to spa businesses alone, but to all projects that promote a balanced lifestyle and awaken your team to a broader perspective of therapies and methods on holistic living.
This can include:

- Music therapist session: http://www.austmta.org.au
- African drumming
- Organised community activities
- Walkathons
- Marathons
- Chakra balancing
- Crystal healing
- Local holistic therapists
- Juice cleanse
- Session with nutritional medicine practitioner
- Local park events
- Yoga
- Cooking classes
- Foot soak sessions: use invites so it doesn't seem like a work environment
- Spa family dinners
- Take time to celebrate holidays and personal achievements

For those living and working in a remote spa setting, giving consideration to the skills that surround you can benefit your team. A trade-off with a chef for a cooking class, or juice cleanses and sessions with guides can transform each team members thinking and appreciation for members outside the spa. Every member has something to share and can shape your therapists to be well-rounded and grounded individuals.

"Leadership is about making others better
as a result of your presence and making
sure that impact lasts in your absence."

—Sheryl Sandberg, COO of Facebook

Balance

Do you think about the spa
when you have a day off?

A well-managed team is reflected by a team
that performs in your absence. And when spa
operations are clear, therapists are focused
on tasks that can be checked on your return,
through the use of checklists.

A Spa Team without a Manager present should
be able to consider the following tasks:

- Self-care: stretch at the beginning of the shift
- Daily cleaning
- Individual training follow up
- Lead group discussion on spa techniques or
  product knowledge

Healthy spa treats

All of the Spa Team should be motivated to be a reflection of spa and wellness. Talk to your team to define what you believe spa and wellness is as a team.

It could be the ability to plan your day around rituals that benefit your body and mind, and nourishing it with nutrient-rich foods, also allowing time to reflect in your own space with breathing exercises.

Carla Oates: The Beauty Chef's Glow Inner Beauty Essential could be a staple in your spa fridge. It is fantastic for gut health and supporting glowing skin and as a quick pick-me-up between treatments on busy days.
www.the beautychef.com

Another favourite is Beauty Bites. Saved for massive days in the spa. The team will be grateful. For the remote Spa it is helpful they are delivered Australia wide.
www.krumbledfoods.com

Importance of self-care

Often written about, and not practised. To give a therapist perspective on the importance of self-care, they often need to be reminded to reflect on how many massages they are giving. To balance that energy, what are they doing for themselves to balance that energy and refuel themselves? As therapists we are often so busy giving that we often forget to receive as well.

Focusing on doable everyday rituals is ideal, and should be discussed with your team.

AM
- Stretch
- Breathing exercises
- Big healthy breakfast/read

PM
- Stretch
- Dry body brush
- Candle with a cup of tea; Dandelion is a favourite

It is ideal to encourage your team to create their own self-care rituals to balance their body as well as their mind.

Many therapists look to their manager for guidance and inspiration. Taking the time to re-evaluate your own daily practices will not only benefit you, but your team as well.

Having an active lifestyle is not a new concept. A healthy lifestyle and keeps you physically and mentally fit for the work that we do. In a remote location some group activities can be difficult to attend on a regular basis. Get involved in the community around you. In remote destinations you explore local events and activities. This can include:

- Hiking
- Swimming
- Tours of local produce makers
- African drumming
- Local therapist: aromatherapy blending workshop
- Music jam sessions
- Visiting Practioner: Naturopath, Osteopath

Mindful practises
- Breathing exercises
- Stretching

Stretching can warm you up for a spa workday, loosen you up at the end and prevent key areas from injury. The routine on the following pages works on major areas, which are used while working in spas. It targets lower back and legs, shoulders and wrists. Feel free you to add to your daily routine.

Stretches

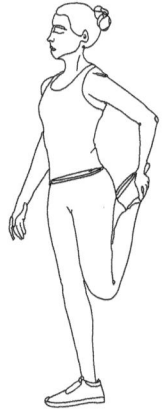

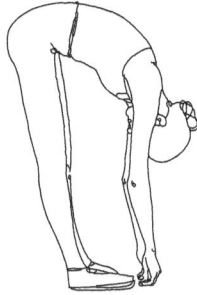

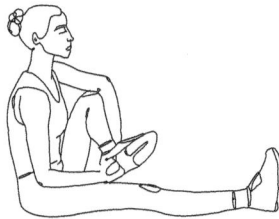

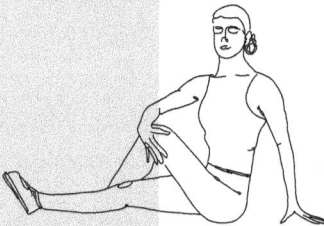

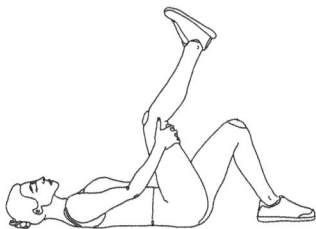

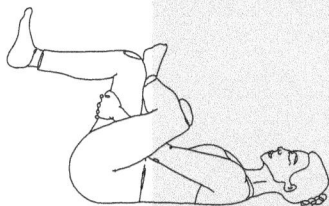

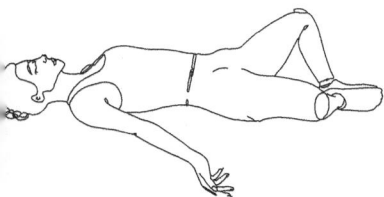

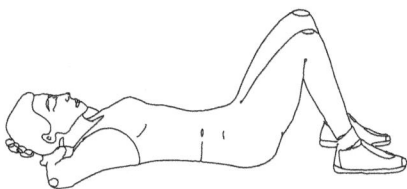

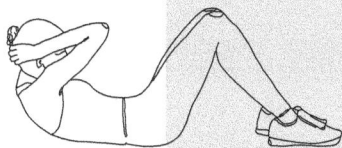

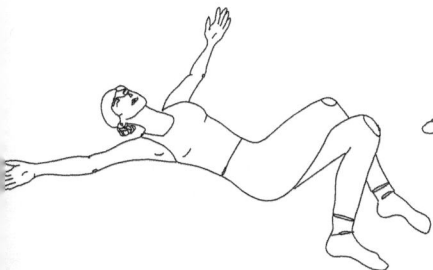

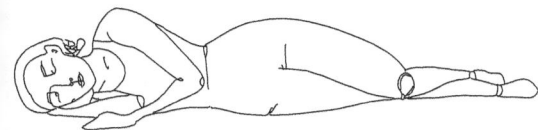

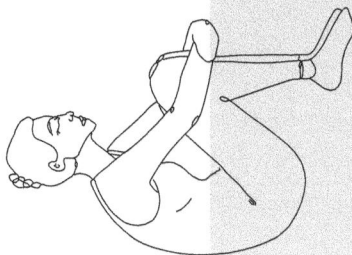

Stretches

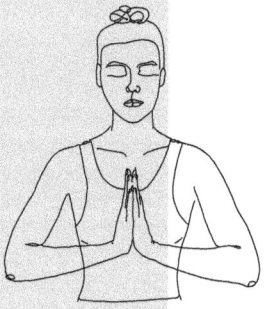
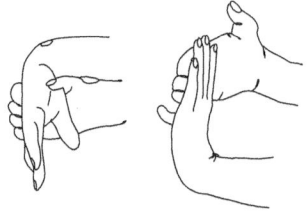

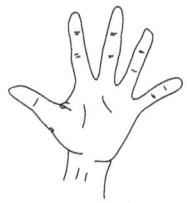
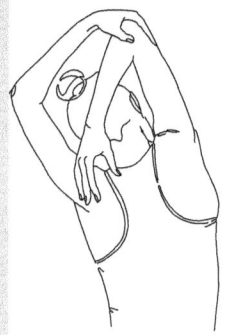

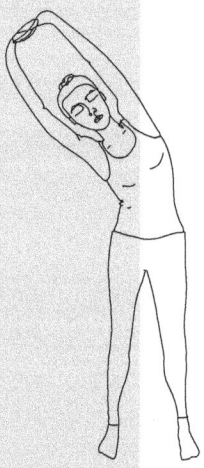
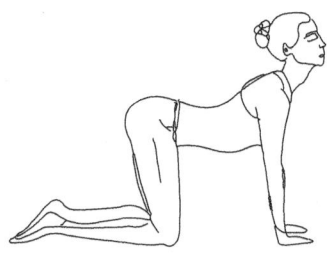

Travel

Many people see travel as an enriching holiday, to learn and see the world from another perspective. Time spent travelling can enable growth for the Spa Therapist, particularly international when time is assigned to explore new spa techniques and see how we have adapted to each other.

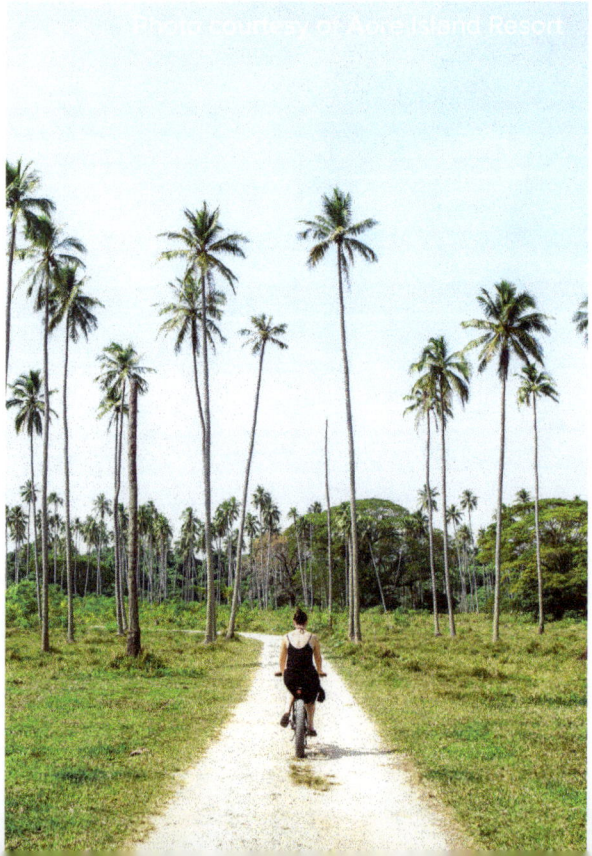

Photo courtesy of Acre Island Resort

"The world is a book and those who do not travel read only one page."

— St Augustine

1.   Australia – Cross Fibre Release/Contractual Tendon Release
2.   Bali – Balinese
3.   Breema — Breemava
4.   China – Gua Sha, Acu-Yoga, Chinese Traditional Medicene, Reflexology
5.   California – Esalen, Watsu Massage
6.   Cambodia – Khmer
7.   Egypt - Aromatherapy
8.   Japan – Shiatsu
9.   Greece – Aromatherapy
10.   India – Aromatherapy, Ayurveda Massage

Do you want to know something really cool?

Ask a question of your team at the end of the day. It leaves them wanting more while being excited for the next shift.

The answer is designed to motivate the team for the next day using positive information delivered in a passionate way.

Give them insight into something you are interested in, a massage technique, a new product that our spa partner is launching, or positive feedback from a guest or higher manager on their efforts.

"True leaders don't create followers...
they create more leaders!"

— J. Sakiya Sandifer, Speaker and Writer #SpaOn

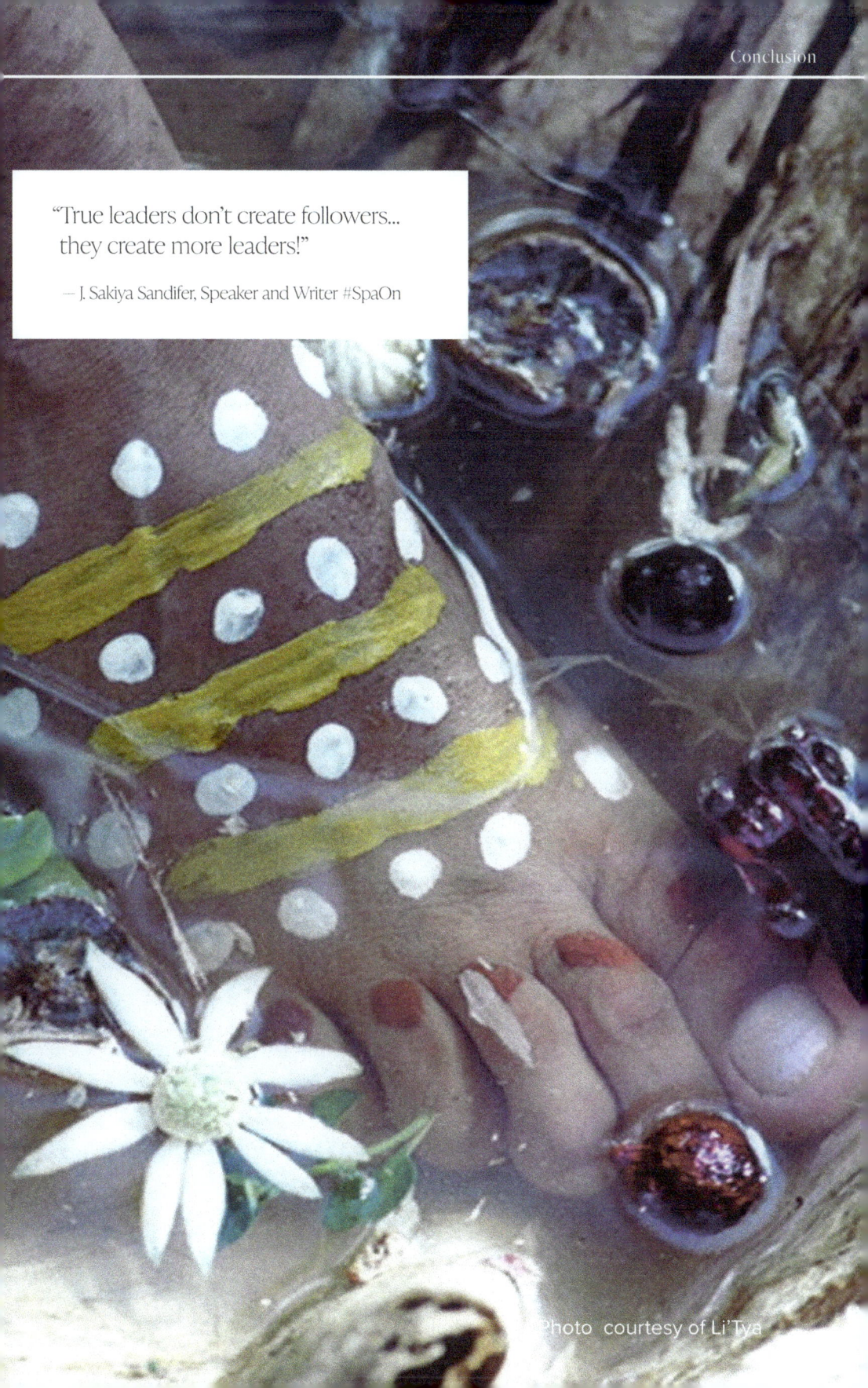

Photo courtesy of Li'Tya

References

Websites

http://www.gobalwellnessinstitute.org/history-of-wellness.com

http://www.discpersonalitytesting.com

http://www.discprofile.com

http://www.musicandimagergy.org.au/Trained-Therapists.html

http://www.thermalbathspa.com/news-info/about-the-spa/spa-history.html

Books

Difficult Personalities, Dr Helen McGrath & Hazel Edwards, 2000, Choice Books, Penguin Random House Australia

Focus, Daniel Goleman, 2013, Bloomsbury Publishing

Harvard Business Essentials, Hiring and Keeping The Best People, 2002, Harvard Business School Publishing Corporation, USA

Personality Plus at Work, Florence Littauer & Rose Sweet, 2011, Revell, Baker Publishing Group

Quiet, Susan Cain, 2012, Crown Publishers

The 7 Habits of Highly Effective People, Steven Covey

The Four Mindsets, Anna-Lucia Mackay, 2015 John Wiley & Sons Australia, Ltd, HCM Global Pty Ltd 2015

The Game Changer: How to use the science of motivation with the power of GAME design to shift behavior, shape culture and make clever happen, Jason A. Fox, 2014, Wiley publishing

Work Smarter: Live Better, Practical ways to change your work habits and transform your life, Cyril Peupion, 2014, Peupion Pty Ltd

Luxury Spa Performance Indicators

Standard	Yes	No
Bookings		
was the guest greeted on arrival at reception?		
was guest name confirmed, not just room number?		
was the treatment clarified, e.g. time and duration?		
if guest had any treatment specific questions, were they given the opportunity to consult with therapist or spa supervisor prior to their appointment?		
did the receptionist give clear explanation of spa's facilities and its location in lodge, if bookings are also taken in main lodge reception also in spa?		
was gender of therapist preference confirmed?		
was the treatment confirmed, including cancellation policy?		
was guest given letter/card with details from reception or advised that it would be delivered by turn down service?		
Spa Service		
was guest welcomed immediately on arrival?		
if not were they aware of policy/welcoming space for them on arrival to wait?		
did the spa employee confirm guest's name/treatment details?		
did the spa employee introduce themselves and offer information on spa/spa partner, and offer spa tour?		
were the facilities available and amenities provided e.g. slippers, gown, disposable underwear, and were they clean?		
during arrival, did spa employee confirm appropriate spa attire required for the treatment?		
did spa employee advise where to go after changing/ where therapist will wait for them?		
did spa employee allow for any questions before treatment, and answer clearly before commencing?		

Standard   Yes   No

The Treatment Session

was the therapist available as per scheduled appointment, if not was acknowledged, and apology offered?

did the therapist introduce themselves and confirm booking details?

did the therapist perform a consultation prior to treatment, detailing medical information and areas of concern/focus?

during consultation did therapist give guest chance to change treatment according to their needs if treatment not appropriate/was a bespoke experience offered?

was privacy offered during disrobing?

was there evidence of hygiene sanitation practices before commencement of treatment?

was the treatment room clean and prepared for the treatment?

did the therapist confirm the comfort of the guest before treatment commencement; temperature of room, level of music, bolster under ankles?

were appropriate draping standards used according to industry standards, and guest's privacy?

did the therapist confirm that the pressure/technique used was comfortable, enjoying the service?

was an eye cover offered for supine position?

was the treatment performed for the allocated duration?

did the therapist inform the guest of the completion of treatment in warm manner while ensuring guest enjoyed the treatment?

was a refreshment offered after the treatment?

did the therapist offer therapy advice/home care advice?

did the therapist suggest another appointment based on guest's needs?

did the therapist advise on how treatment will be billed, if straight to their room or otherwise?

did the therapist offer a space for further relaxation?

did the therapist offer a sequence of events, if they weren't available to stay with guest e.g. locker shown, how long they can stay?

Standard	Yes	No

The Treatment Session

did the therapist thank the guest for coming to the spa?

did the therapist inform guest on how to contact spa/therapist for further treatments or advice before departure?

The Spa Therapist

was the therapist genuine and warm in their speech and body language?

was the therapist's interactions with other staff positive and reflection of the relaxing environment?

was the therapist neat and taking pride in their appearance and uniform?

did the therapist speak clearly, free from scripted text and jargon?

was the therapist confident and passionate engaging in treatment and therapy advice?

did the therapist detail their own qualifications/specialty?

did the therapist offer intuitive service?

did therapist have a thorough knowledge of spa and lodge?

was the spa journey and interactions personalised?

did therapist offer solutions where challenges arose with clear communication and care?

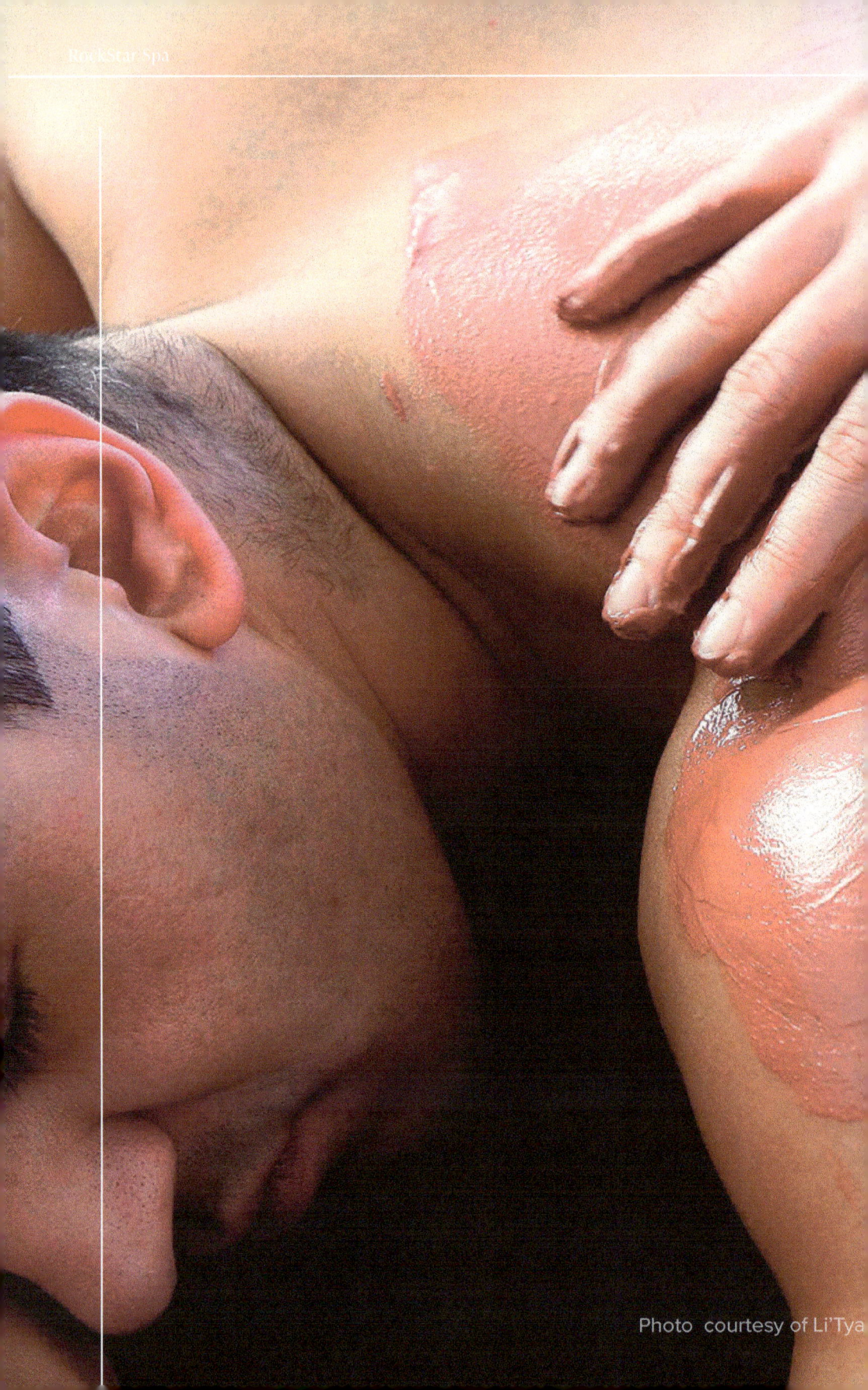

RockStar Development Program

Standard	Topic	Duration
Specialisation	• Understanding therapist's own skillset • Confidence • Develop own Mission Statement	30 mins
Industry Awareness	• Therapists • Therapy/Techniques • Products • How my skillset fits in • How my current spa product fits in with what people are using • Retail vs Upselling vs Rebooking, how to decipher the best option for your guests while maintaining your budget target.	60 mins
Language	• Correct use of English/no jargon • Spa speak • Body language, voice volume, speaking with hands • Conversational vs lecture • Quality information: client not a blank slate	30 mins
Self-Care	• Daily rituals • Strength and conditioning • Balance, every day do something just for you • Holidays	30 mins
Action Plan	• Mentor • Further study • Manager's feed	30 mins

Timing Table

Fill out your own Timing Table below to get into mindful time management habits. It can be copied and used as a daily action plan.
Note how many of your tasks are important compared to urgent.

Date	Tasks to Action

15 Mins

☐ Important
☐ Urgent

☐ Important
☐ Urgent

☐ Important
☐ Urgent

60 Mins

☐ Important
☐ Urgent

☐ Important
☐ Urgent

☐ Important
☐ Urgent

☐ Important
☐ Urgent

90 Mins

☐ Important
☐ Urgent

☐ Important
☐ Urgent

☐ Important
☐ Urgent

Daily Operations Checklist

Action Required	S	M	T	W	T	F	S

Open spa

Check linen delivery

Turn on lights, music, hot cabbies

Phone checked for messages,
and reply if action required

Turn on steam room and sauna

Ensure steam room and sauna has
refreshments and towels stocked

Brew tea of day

Fill water stations

Amenities fully stocked in bathrooms

Plump cushions in lounge

Sweep front entrance

Treatment rooms stocked with
fibrella/cotton rounds

All surfaces in treatment rooms
clear of visible oil marks

BOH tidy

Appointment book checked, day
printed for therapise BOH prep area

POS system turned on ready payments

Close Spa

Next day appointments confirmed

End of day report/reciepts cash up

Turn off hot cabbies, leave door open,
empty trays of excess water

Turn off steam room and sauna

Spray steam with disinfectant

Clean/refresh bathroom lockers, top
up all amenities, towels, combs etc.

Empty all bins

Clean and put away all equipment used

Wipe BOH benches, Ecolab green spray

Clean all teacups and put away

Turn off music/lights

Linen in bags, to BOH entrance for pickup

Lock all doors

Spa amenities and tools checklist

Action Required   S   M   T   W   T   F   S

Amenities - from laundry

Candles

Tissues

Toilet Paper

Refill all shampoo, conditioner, bodywash.

Hand wash and body lotion whole new container, no refill

From ALM store, key required

Cotton rounds

Cotton tips

Tissue box covers - in case of breakage

Bins - in case of breakage

Tea cups - in case of breakage

Cleaning Equipment - from laundry

Mop heads

Sponges

Glass cleaner - blue spray, refill

Bathroom cleaner - pink spray refill

Disinfectant deodorizer - green spray, refill

Dishwashing liquid, refill

From kitchen

Floor cleaner

Sanitiser (for steam and equipment)

Office Supplies - from FO BOH

Brown retail bags - small

Guest collateral, media pamphlets

Guest notepads and pens

Printer paper

Printer cartridge

Goal setting

| GOAL | What I want to achieve |

| MEASURE FOR THIS ACHIEVEMENT | Subjective measures; facts
Objective measures; how you feel about goal now |

| DATE TO ACCOMPLISH BY | Timeline to complete goal |

| WHAT WILL I NEED TO ACCOMPLISH MY GOAL | Resources, Training, Funds, Mentoring |

| IS MY GOAL ACHIEVABLE | Is what I want attainable, can I make this happen myself? |

| WHAT ACTIONS DO I NEED TO DO | 1.
2.
3.
4.
5. |

| STEPS REQUIRED TO COMPLETE ACTION | 1.
2.
3.
4.
5. |

Luxury spa performance indicators

Standard	Yes	No

Bookings

was the guest greeted on arrival at reception?

was guest name confirmed, not just room number?

was the treatment clarified, e.g. time and duration?

if guest had any treatment specific questions, where they given the opportunity to consult with therapist or spa supervisor prior to their appointment?

did the receptionist give clear explanation of spa's facilities and its location in lodge, if bookings are also taken in main lodge reception also in spa?

was gender of therapist preference confirmed?

was the treatment confirmed, including cancellation policy?

was guest given letter/card with details from reception or advised that it would be delivered by turn down service?

Spa Service

was guest welcomed immediately on arrival?

if not were they aware of policy/welcoming space for them on arrival to wait?

did the spa employee confirm guests name/treatment details?

did the spa employee introduce themselves and offer information on spa/spa partner, and offer spa tour?

where the facilities available and amenities provided e.g. slippers, gown, disposable underwear, and were they clean?

during arrival, did spa employee confirm appropriate spa attire required for the treatment?

did spa employee advise where to go after changing/ where therapist will wait for them?

did spa employee allow for any questions before treatment, and answer clearly before commencing?

Standard	Yes	No

The Treatment Session

was the therapist available as per scheduled appointment, if not was acknowledged, and apology offered?

did the therapist introduce themselves and confirm booking details?

did the therapist perform a consultation prior to treatment, detailing medical information and areas of concern/focus?

during consultation did therapist give guest chance to change treatment according to their needs if treatment not appropriate/was a bespoke experience offered?

was privacy offered during disrobing?

was there evidence of hygiene sanitation practices before commencement of treatment?

was the treatment room clean and prepared for the treatment?

did the therapist confirm the comfort of the guest before treatment commencement; temperature of room, level of music, bolster under ankles?

were appropriate draping standards used according to industry standards, and guests privacy?

did the therapist confirm that the pressure/technique used was comfortable, enjoying the service?

was an eye cover offered for supine position?

was the treatment performed for the allocated duration?

did the therapist inform the guest of the completion of treatment in warm manner while ensuring guest enjoyed the treatment?

was a refreshment offered after the treatment?

did the therapist offer therapy advice/home care advice?

did the therapist suggest another appointment based on guests needs?

did the therapist advise on how treatment will be billed, if straight to their room or otherwise?

did the therapist offer a space for further relaxation?

did the therapist offer a sequence of events, if they weren't available to stay with guest e.g. locker shown, how long they can stay?

Standard	Yes	No

The Treatment Session

did the therapist thank the guest for coming to the spa?

did the therapist inform guest on how to contact spa/ therapist for further treatments or advice before departure?

The Spa Therapist

was the therapist genuine and warm in their speech and body language?

was the therapist's interactions with other staff positive and reflection of the relaxing environment?

was the therapist neat and taking pride in their appearance and uniform?

did the therapist speak clearly, free from scripted text and jargon?

was the therapist confident and passionate engaging in treatment and therapy advice?

did the therapist detail their own qualifications/specialty?

did the therapist offer intuitive service?

did therapist have a thorough knowledge of spa and lodge?

was the spa journey and interactions personalised?

did therapist offer solutions where challenges arose with clear communication and care?

Acknowledgments

Thank you to Hayley and James Baillie of Baillie Lodges for allowing me to include photos of Southern Spa, Southern Ocean Lodge and Spa Kinara, Longitude 131°.

The warmest thank you to Anne Warren from Li'Tya, (meaning 'of the earth') for her specialist spa training. Li'Tya is a spa brand powered by Australian native botanicals inspired by Australian Aborignal wisdom.

Thank you to Bryan McGoldrick and Jill Coughlan of Li'Tya, who read initial drafts of RockStar Spa, and were very encouraging. Thank for your support and recommending that I proceed with the publication of RockStar Spa.

Thank you to Li'Tya for the beautiful photos scattered throughout the pages of this book.

Thank you to Brad, Lisa, and Montana Gray from Aore Island Resort for allowing me to share their topical resort.

This project may have taken much longer to get off the ground without the assistance of Corrie Gardner who was able to point me in the right direction. I am very grateful for her guidance.

Thank you to Suzanne Haddon and the team at Rooland for the front cover and giving the pages of RockStar Spa life.

Many thanks to Michael Hanrahan and the Publish Central team for being so patient with a novice and for their support, editing and publishing.

Many thanks to Jeanette Gray for her ongoing support and being my biggest fan.

I would like to acknowledge all my spa teams from my career of 15 years. Thank you for sharing your knowledge, passion and friendship in this caring and healing industry that we all love so much.

#spaon